Mary Ann Devos presents...

Exceptional Works
In Metal Clay & Glass

Wardell
PUBLICATIONS INC

Cataloguing in Publication Data

Mary Ann Devos

Exceptional Works In Metal Clay & Glass

     ISBN-13: 978-0-919985-56-8

     ISBN-10: 0-919985-56-4

1. Jewelry making 2. Metal Clay.

I. Devos, Ken   II. Title

TH8271.F73 2008   748.509795'49   C2008-907062-0

Printed in Thailand by Phongwarin Printing Ltd.

Published simultaneously in Canada and USA

E-mail: info@wardellpublications.com

Website: www.wardellpublications.com

Mary Ann Devos presents...

Exceptional Works
In Metal Clay & Glass

Creative Direction & Project Coordination
Mary Ann Devos & Ken Devos

Photography
Ken Devos

Contributing Artists
See page 5

Book Layout & Typography
Randy Wardell

Text Transcribed & Edited by
Randy Wardell

Special Thanks

We enjoy our work with PMC Connection and Mikuni American, who have served as a direct importer of Precious Metal Clay to the United States. They have provided us the opportunity to use and teach PMC techniques across the US as well as abroad. We thank the wonderful people at Mikuni: Mr. Satoshi Fugimori, President, Mr. Shige Ikuta, Exec. VP, Mr. Dennis Nakashima, VP, Michele Tsuzuki, Crystal Swandjaja and Margaret Flynn, office staff and at PMC Connection: Earl Roberts and Vondell Wallis (recently retired).

We thank Mitsubishi Materials Corporation for developing PMC and for their continuing work to introduce new forms of the material. We are grateful for their support for PMC and PMC education in the US and across the world.

We are very proud to work with a great team of talented and hard working Senior Teachers who share their passion for art and PMC with everyone they meet. We cannot thank them enough for all their efforts and support. It was also a great privilege to work with all the Art Clay artists supported by Art Clay World USA and Aida Chemical Corp Ltd.

It was very difficult selecting the pieces to present in this book. There is so much creativity demonstrated by the artists within the metal clay community. We want this book to celebrate the best artists using metal clay. They continue to expand the applications of silver clay as an artistic medium, making new discoveries daily and bringing this new material to the forefront of the "Art of Adornment" movement.

Published by

PUBLICATIONS INC

To receive our electronic newsletter or to send suggestions please contact us by e-mail: info@wardellpublications.com or visit our Website: www.wardellpublications.com

About Mary Ann & Ken Devos

Mary Ann is a pioneer in metal clay and has worked with it since 1996. She was the Director of Education for Art Clay and now is the Director of Education for PMC Connection, a direct importer of PMC into the US. In those positions, she created the education programs for those companies. The PMC Connection Certification program has been very successful here and abroad. In her current position she leads a fantastic group of Senior Teachers, spreading the joy of silver clay.

Mary Ann & Ken have collaborated on two books for PMC titled: 'Introduction to Precious Metal Clay' and 'Precious Metal Clay in Mixed Media', both published by Wardell Publications Inc. In addition they have had the privilege to teach metal clay techniques in Europe, Japan, South Africa, Australia, Canada, and across the USA.

Ken is the Program Coordinator and a Senior Teacher for PMC Connection. In addition to teaching PMC techniques as a team with Mary Ann, he is responsible for the business end of the process. He served as Senior Editor and provided photography for both of Mary Ann's first two books. He has continued this effort in this newest work.

A Note from Mary Ann & Ken:

We are life partners as well as a metal clay team and we are proud to say that we have been married for 39 years (as of 2008). Art has been a major focus in our lives and working together as metal clay artists and teachers is our passion.

Over the years, we have shared some wonderful experiences. We have been blessed with two beautiful daughters who, in turn, have brought into our lives their husbands and our four grandchildren. All through our married lives, we have enhanced our professional careers with liberal sprinklings of artistic activities. No matter what or where we happened to find ourselves, some creative outlet usually was close at hand.

Metal clay is a material in its infancy. It is hard to believe how far artists have taken it since it was first introduced to the US in 1996. As we travel across North America and around the world to present silver clay classes it's amazing to see what these artists have been able to create.

When we started planning this book with Randy (the Publisher) we wanted to showcase the most exciting objects we could find and to celebrate the artists who created them. Our idea was to present the metal clay art the same way a person might view a piece if they had it in their hand - from every angle. One of Ken's passions is photography and getting just the right lighting and arrangements for each project.

We hope that you enjoy the work presented in this book and that you are as inspired by these works as we have been. All pieces presented in this book combine silver clay with some form of glass. We believe that they all demonstrate the creative potential available by the use of these two materials in the same project. The greatest aspect of these pieces, however, is the knowledge that we are just beginning to explore the possible uses of silver clay as an artistic material. We are privileged to have this opportunity to work with this group of metal clay and glass artists. It is our hope that you will join us on this creative adventure.

Mary Ann & Ken Devos

Contact Information

Mary Ann & Ken Devos

Website: www.silverclayworks.com

Website: www.exceptionalworks.net

Table of Contents:

The 'Exceptional Works' Showcase Galleries

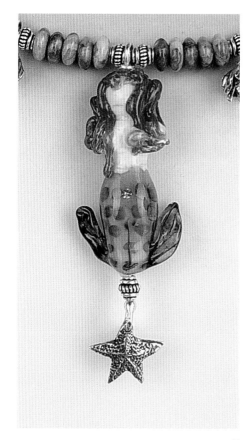

Metal Clay - The Raw Material

As the title of this book suggests every project in this book uses a material that goes by the generic term 'Metal Clay'. But what is metal clay and where did it come from? Mitsubishi Materials Corporation of Japan developed a material in the early 1990's that can be molded and worked very much like porcelain clay and after it is fired in a kiln all that is left is solid fine silver. Mitsubishi received a patent for that product in 1994. They called their product line "Precious Metal Clay" and introduced it to the United States in 1996. This material was followed in 1998 by a competing product called Art Clay Silver, produced and marketed by Aida Chemical Industries, Co., Ltd., also of Japan.

Brooch (see page 53) with metal clay extrusions

What is Metal Clay?

Silver clay consists of fine silver (.999 pure) in a powdered form, an organic fiber binder and water. Gold clay uses 22 K gold powder that is an alloy of 24 K gold and .999 fine silver. Since the binder and water are burned off completely in the firing process, the resultant metals can be hallmarked as .999 (silver) or 22 K gold. Silver clay comes in four forms: lump clay, paste clay, syringe clay and sheet clay; gold clay is available only in lump clay form.

Easily mold lump type metal clay using your fingers

How does Metal Clay Work?

The binder and water in these clays are present simply to hold the metal powders in a pliable form. The user sculpts with the metal clay by shaping, drying and finishing the piece in a process very similar to molding potters clay. When the piece is completely dry, it is fired, usually with a small jewelry kiln but often with a small butane torch or a specialty kiln such as the SpeedFire Cone or Hot Pot. The heat of the firing process drives off any residual water, burns off the fiber binder and causes the metal powder to sinter (fuse together without changing shape). When properly fired, the sintered metal has a density and strength very close to that of cast fine silver. The fired metals can be polished using traditional metalsmithing techniques.

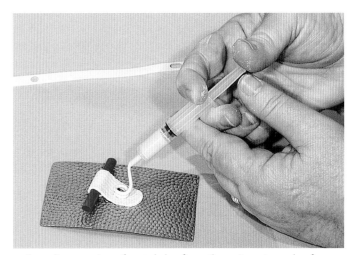

Extruding a string of metal clay from the syringe type clay form

How Is It Manipulated

In the clay form, the material is very malleable, similar to ceramic clay. Due to the metal clay's advanced technology, the artist is able to shape the material, using a wide range of tools from sophisticated shapers to one's own fingers. The lump clay can be shaped using traditional slab and coil forming techniques while the syringe clay is extruded through a narrow nozzle providing a shape similar to wire. The paste form is used to join two or more other clay components into more complex sculptural forms. Paste can also be used to create an exact replica of a natural organic form, such as a leaf or a twig. The paste is painted on the item and when fired the organic material burns off leaving the shape and texture of the original natural item. Sheet clay is similar in feel to a sheet of vinyl. It can be cut, folded or laminated to create interesting silver shapes.

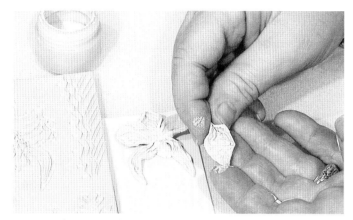

Sculpting a 3-dimensional orchid using lump type clay

What Is The Firing Process?

Because the unfired clay material is a combination of metal powder, binder and water, the firing process causes the form to shrink as the water evaporates, the binder burns off and the metal powder sinters, usually about 10-14% from the dried and unfired form. The exact amount of shrinkage depends in part upon the temperature and length of the firing. Precious Metal Clay types fire within a range of 1110°F / 600°C (for 45 minutes) to 1650°F / 900°C (for 10 to 120 minutes depending upon the clay type.) Art Clay Silver fires within a range of 1202°F / 650°C to 1598°F / 870°C (for 10 to 30 minutes depending upon the clay type.)

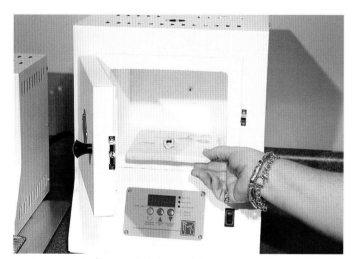

Preparing to fire a metal clay sculpture in a small jewelry kiln

Combine Other Materials and Metal Clay

The variety of clay types also provides a range of firing temperatures and times, making the material suitable for use in combination with a variety of other materials. Some items, such as lab grown gemstones and CZ's (cubic zirconia)

will withstand the highest silver clay firing temperatures, while other materials such as glass work better at the lowest temperatures. Since most of these materials are more sensitive to temperature than time, the longer time requirement at a recommended lower temperature does not appear to affect them.

Some materials such as ceramics will take even greater heat than the silver clays so that adding the silver after the ceramic has been fired allows the use of a lower firing temperature for the silver and still allows the silver to "shrink wrap" itself closely to the ceramic material. Still other materials such as some natural gemstones will accept the lowest silver clay firing temperatures.

Pendant (see page 12), metal clay combined with dichroic glass

It looks Like a Lot Of Fun!

All of the metal clays can be used to create beautiful precious metal objects with a minimum of tools and expensive equipment. Whether you use a computer controlled jewelry kiln, a pyrometer gauged kiln, a fuel kiln such as the Hot Pot or the SpeedFire Cone or even a butane torch, you can start with a relatively small investment in materials and equipment and finish with unique silver artwork.

There now are several excellent books on the market that will take you through the entire process from collecting supplies to polishing the finished pieces. Two of these books are published by Wardell Publications Inc (also publisher of the book you're reading now) they are: Introduction to Precious Metal Clay and Precious Metal Clay in Mixed Media, both written by Mary Ann Devos.

Symmetry In Motion

Kaleidoscope and Truck Stand

Alice Alper-Rein

Morganville, New Jersey USA
www.jewelrybyy2a.com

In addition to creating wearable art Alice Alper-Rein enjoys the challenge of 'thinking outside the jewelry box' to create larger kinetic structures using metal clay. Mechanisms that produce motion, sound and/or reflect light are enclosed within the metal clay body. These miniatures works-of-art excite the senses and add new possibilities of what can be created with metal clay.

Physical Attributes

- Kaleidoscope:
  1" (2.5 cm) High
  3/4" (19 mm) Wide
  3" (7.6 cm) Long
- Truck Stand: 2" (5.1 cm) High
  3/4" (19 mm) Wide
  5 5/8" (14.3 cm) Long

Materials & Components

- Lump clay & Paste clay
- Brass, Sterling Silver, Zinc & Stainless Steel
- Cubic zirconia
- Fusible & Dichroic Glass
- Kaleidoscope parts, (optical lenses & front surface mirrors)

Way Over The Rainbow
A Musical Kaleidoscope

Alice Alper-Rein
Morganville, New Jersey USA
www.jewelrybyy2a.com

When the colorful, fused glass object wheel of this combination kaleidoscope/music box is wound, it plays 'Somewhere Over the Rainbow'. A peek through the kaleidoscope reveals the ever-changing dichroic patterns that are excitingly "Way Over The Rainbow". The kaleidoscope easily swings out of the way to enable the exchange of alternate theme color wheels.

Physical Attributes

- 4 1/2" (11.5 cm) High
- 2" (5.1 cm) Wide
- 3 3/8" (8.6 cm) Long

Materials & Components

- Lump clay & Paste clay
- Brass & Sterling Silver
- Fusible & Dichroic Glass
- Kaleidoscope parts, (optical lenses
- & front surface mirrors)
- Music Box Mechanism

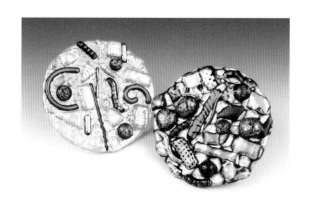

Interchangeable alternate theme color wheels

Eastern Star

Lidded Box & Pendant Combination

Linda Bernstein

Bonny Doon, California USA
www.artique.org

Linda's work uses a synthesis of ancient symbols and techniques to blend the past with present day materials (metal clay) to create a bridge to the future. This 'Eastern Star' piece features a gently curved shape that was inspired by travel to Asia. The stars represent the eastern light of hope. The curved box lid is actually a pendant complete with necklace chain that is hidden inside the box. This piece has several surprise elements to delight the viewer that include a shooting star, a heart shaped charm clasp and a star floating in the glass enamel.

Physical Attributes

- Box:
  7/8" (22 mm) High
  3/4" (19 mm) Wide
  1 5/8" (4.1 cm) Long
- Box Lid/Pendant:
  1" (2.5 cm) Wide
  2" (5.1 cm) Long

Materials & Components

- Lump clay & Paste clay
- Sterling Silver neck chain
- Sterling Silver chain clasp
- Glass Enamel

Japanesque Butterflies
Twin Butterfly Pendant Necklace

Olivia Competente
San Francisco, California USA
www.jewelsbyolivia.com

Olivia loves to add color to her pieces using unleaded glass enamels to give depth and vibrancy to the metal. She looks to nature for inspiration adding "Butterflies have always been special to me because they represent free spirits that guide the soul." This twin feature necklace has the look and feel of jewelry out of a fairy tale from a bygone era. The colors were derived from a Japanese block print and the shape is a tribute to the art nouveau movement.

Physical Attributes

- Butterfly Pendant:
  1 1/2" (3.8 cm) Wide
  2" (5.1 cm) Long
- Necklace Centerpiece:
  3 1/2" (9 cm) High
  4" (10.2 cm) Wide
- Beaded Chains:
  6" (15.2 cm) Long (each)
- Silver Chain:
  11" (28 cm) Long

Materials & Components

- Lump, Paste & Syringe clay
- Cubic zirconia stones
- Sterling Silver chain & clasp
- Austrian Crystal necklace
- Glass Enamel

Green Glamour
Silver & Dichroic Cabochon Pendant

Babette Cox
Dallas, Texas USA
www.babettecox.com

Barbara McGuire, (Oval Frame Rubber Stamp)
Buford, Georgia USA
www.barbaramcguire.com

Working with metal clay & glass makes Babette's world come alive. The oval frame rubber stamp set the size and shape for the pendant and the brilliant dichroic cabochon led the way for the colors in the multi-stranded necklace. The cabochon is secured using two strings of syringe clay, augmenting the embossed work on the pendant base.

Physical Attributes
- Pendant:
  2" (5.1 cm) Wide
  2 1/8" (5.4 cm) High
  1/2" (13 mm) Thick
- Necklace (overall):
  13 1/2" (34.3 cm) Hanging Length

Materials & Components
- Lump, Paste & Syringe clay
- Dichroic glass cabochon
- Sterling Silver clasp & cones
- Glass, crystal & metal beads

Source of Life

Pate de verre Glass & Silver Pendant

Ann Davis

Springfield, Virginia USA
www.anndavisstudio.com

Archaeology has always been a cornerstone of Ann's work. She states, "I love my work to have that 'just unearthed' feeling. When I see vessels in museums I always think of the hand of the potter that fashioned it". This 'Source of Life' pendant depicts the hand of 'Gaia' (Greek goddess personifying the Earth) pouring out the waters of life from an emblematic vessel. You can see the watery spirals on the vase and bail along with a kelp forest embossing on the front side of the pate de verre vase.

Physical Attributes

- Pendant:
  3 1/2" (8.9 cm) High
  2" (5.1 cm) Wide
- Necklace (Overall):
  18" (46 cm) Cord Length
  9 1/2" (24 cm) Hanging Length

Materials & Components

- Lump clay & Paste clay
- Pate de verre glass mix
- Silicone Air tube neck cord
- Patina

Night Time, Light Time
Silver, Copper & Fused Glass Sculpture

Ken Devos

Fort Myers Beach, Florida USA
www.silverclayworks.com

Ken has used a variety of artistic media to express his creative point of view. Most recently he has concentrated on the use of silver in the form of metal clay plus fine silver wire and chain. The artist comments, "The meeting of water and land has always held an attraction for me. For this piece I wanted to explore how the geometric shapes of the lighthouse buildings provided a link to the more organic form of the fused glass base." The base was created with multiple layers of glass to provide a contrast of colors to offset the shape.

Physical Attributes

- 2 1/4" (5.7 cm) High
- 3" (7.6 cm) Wide
- 4" (10.2 cm) Long

Materials & Components

- Lump & Paste clay
- Copper sheet
- Fused & Blown Glass

Guardian of Mount Edna

Silver, Glass & Lava Bead Necklace

Mary Ann Devos
Fort Myers Beach, Florida USA
www.silverclayworks.com

Mary Ann was on a tour of Sicily in 2004 while Mount Edna was spewing ash. It was a mystical moment to experience first hand the creation of new stone from the center of the earth. The artist comments, "We collected lava beads at a street market and when I got back to my studio I worked on a series of goddess figures that pay tribute to the beautiful water that surrounds the island. The lava beads remind us of how precarious life can be on this exquisite island."

Physical Attributes

- Pendant:
  3 1/2" (8.9 cm) Long
  1" (2.5 cm) Wide
  1/4" (6 mm) Thick
- Necklace (Overall):
  20" (51 cm) Cord Length
  9 1/4" (23.5 cm) Hanging Length

Materials & Components

- Lump, Paste & Syringe clay
- Dichroic Glass
- Fine Silver Wire
- Sicilian Lava Beads
- Glass & Silver Beads

Mermaid Dreams

Flameworked Bead & Silver Necklace

Mary Ann Devos

Fort Myers Beach, Florida USA
www.silverclayworks.com

Judy Peppers, (Glass Mermaid Bead)

Brasstown, North Carolina, USA
www.judypeppers.com

Judy Peppers is a very talented glass bead artist. She studied metal clay techniques at one of Mary Ann's classes. Some time later they decided to collaborate. Judy created the mermaid pendant and the fish beads and Mary Ann took it from there. Mary Ann comments, "It was fun to design sea flowers and shells in silver to go with the glass mermaid and fish. When it was time to create the necklace itself I found these wonderful jasper stone beads that go perfectly with the colors in the mermaid."

Physical Attributes

- Pendant:
  2 3/8" (6 cm) High
  (3 1/2" (9 cm) including star)
  1 1/4" (3.2 cm) Wide
  3/4" (19 mm) Deep
- Necklace (Overall):
  18" (46 cm) Cord Length
  9 1/2" (24 cm) Hanging Length

Materials & Components

- Lump, Paste & Syringe clay
- Flameworked Glass Beads
- Sterling Silver beads
- Jasper Stone beads

Spirit of the Sea

Glass Beads & Silver Brooch

Mary Ann Devos

Fort Myers Beach, Florida USA
www.silverclayworks.com

For Mary Ann silver clay opens up more creative options than any other art medium that she has worked with. Masks have a particular fascination for her. A walk with her granddaughter CeCe inspired the shell embellishments used on this mask. The artist comments, "CeCe & I collected these wonderful tiny shells from the beach. We took them back to my studio, made rubber molds with them and then created silver shells using metal clay. I worked with sheet clay, laminated to 4 thicknesses, to create the face, then used lump and syringe clay to decorate it. Stringing glass and pearl beads on silver wire created the fantastically wild hair."

Physical Attributes

- 3" (7.6 cm) Long
- 2 1/4" (5.7 cm) Wide
- 1/2" (13 mm) Thick

Materials & Components

- Lump, Paste & Syringe clay
- Fine Silver Wire
- Glass & Pearl Beads

Silver & Flameworked Glass Pendant

Mary Ann Devos
Fort Myers Beach, Florida USA
www.silverclayworks.com

Sharon Peters, (Flameworked Glass Beads)
Alameda, California USA
www.smartassglass.com

Sharon is known for her whimsical beads that are so much fun that you just have to smile when you see them. Mary Ann met Sharon at a bead show and they decided to collaborate on a glass & silver project. Mary Ann comments, "I was thrilled to work with Sharon. She offered her chicken & eggs bead set titled 'Poultry in Motion' and I added the silver feedbag, the chicks and clucks tubes and other assorted beads." Let the Chicken Dance begin!

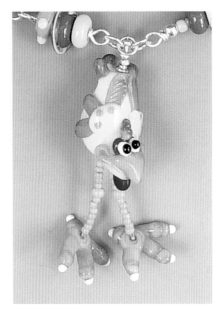

Physical Attributes
- Pendant:
  2 1/4" (5.7 cm) High
  1 1/4" (3.2 cm) Wide
  3/4" (19 mm) Deep
- Necklace (Overall):
  24" (61 cm) Cord Length
  11 3/4" (30 cm) Hanging Length

Materials & Components
- Lump, Paste & Syringe clay
- Flameworked Glass Beads
- Silver & Glass seed beads
- Fine Silver wire

Blue Moon Flower
Silver & Glass Enamel Pendant

Mary Ann Devos

Fort Myers Beach, Florida USA
www.silverclayworks.com

Flowers are a frequent thread in Mary Ann's jewelry designs. This particular flower is not a direct copy of a flower found in nature, rather it is an interpretation of an orchid shape that has a structure and color all its own. The artist comments, "Metal clay is a wonderful base for glass enamels. I like to draw the cloisions (raised partitions) using syringe work and then fire and polish the fine silver. Then I add the enamels and fire the piece again."

Physical Attributes

- Pendant:
  1 3/4" (4.4 cm) High
  2" (5.1 cm) Wide
  1/2" (13 mm) Deep
- Necklace (Overall):
  20" (51 cm) Cord Length
  8 1/2" (21.5 cm) Hanging Length

Materials & Components

- Lump, Paste & Syringe clay
- Lab grown Sapphire
- Glass Enamels
- Sterling Silver beads
- Glass Beads

Layered Cake Ring
Silver & Glass Cabochon Ring

Mary Ann Devos

Fort Myers Beach, Florida USA
www.silverclayworks.com

Mary Ann's designs are often influenced by the art of ancient cultures and this hollow form ring has a definite historic flavor. Mary Ann comments, "For me, building a hollow form on top of a band style ring is a lot of fun because it come together quickly and looks fabulous. I used a dichroic cabochon created by Pacific Art Glass as the 'icing' for this cake-shaped ring that is meant to be a celebration of life."

Physical Attributes

- 1 1/4" (3.2 cm) High
- 5/8" (16 mm) Wide

Materials & Components

- Lump & Sheet clay
- Dichroic Glass cabochon

Journey Book Pendant
Silver, Mother of Pearl & Glass Pendant

Journey Book Pendant
Silver, Mother of Pearl & Glass Pendant

Mary Ann Devos
Fort Myers Beach, Florida USA
www.silverclayworks.com

Ken Devos, (Sterling Silver & Bead Chain)
Fort Myers Beach, Florida USA
www.silverclayworks.com

The book pendant is an update to the more traditional memory locket pendant. This one has silver front cover and a mother of pearl back plate. Mary Ann comments, "It's great to make jewelry that is ultimately a wearable keepsake. This book style pendant features silver clay beach shells and a heart cutout that frames a detail in the photo of our daughters that is mounted on the inside."

Physical Attributes

- Pendant:
  3" (7.6 cm) High
  2" (5.1 cm) Wide
  1/4" (6 mm) Thick
- Necklace (Overall):
  20" (51 cm) Cord Length
  8 1/2" (21.6 cm) Hanging Length

Materials & Components

- Lump, Paste & Syringe clay
- Mother of Pearl
- Dichroic Glass Beads
- Sterling Silver wire

Golden Slipper Orchid

Silver & Glass Enamels Pendant

Mary Ann Devos

Fort Myers Beach, Florida USA
www.silverclayworks.com

Mary Ann integrates a lot of flower designs in her work and orchids are one of her favorite. This pendant was fabricated using a 3 dimensional technique that gives it a very realistic look. The artist comments, "To me orchids are elegant and sensual. The enamels allow me to add color and the gold gives a sparkle to the overall composition."

Physical Attributes

- Pendant:
  1 1/2" (3.8 cm) High
  1 1/2" (3.8 cm) Wide
  3/8" (10 mm) Thick
- Necklace (Overall):
  22" (56 cm) Cord Length
  9" (23 cm) Hanging Length

Materials & Components

- Lump, Paste & Syringe clay
- 22K Gold Paste clay
- Glass Enamels
- Crystal glass Beads
- Sterling Silver Beads

Memories Of Australia
Silver, Leather & Dichroic Glass Pendant

Mary Ann Devos
Fort Myers Beach, Florida USA
www.silverclayworks.com

Ken Devos, (Sterling Silver Chain)
Fort Myers Beach, Florida USA
www.silverclayworks.com

Mary Ann loves to mix it up with mixed media in her Jewelry creations. For this piece she has combined silver, leather, dichroic glass created by Pacific Art Glass, sterling silver, and photography. Mary Ann comments, "Mixed media is always fun – the possibilities are endless. This keepsake pendant is a reminder of our trip to Australia where we met many wonderful artists and had a great time."

Physical Attributes

- Pendant:
  2 1/2" (6.4 cm) High
  1 1/2" (3.8 cm) Wide
  1/4" (6 mm) Thick
- Necklace (Overall):
  22" (56 cm) Cord Length
  10 1/2" (27 cm) Hanging Length

Materials & Components

- Lump, Paste & Syringe clay
- Leather & Photos
- Dichroic Glass Cabochon
- Sterling Silver Wire

Victorian Garden Box

Silver, Dichroic Glass & Sapphire Pendant

Mary Ann Devos

Fort Myers Beach, Florida USA
www.silverclayworks.com

Ken Devos, (Sterling Silver Chain)

Fort Myers Beach, Florida USA
www.silverclayworks.com

Mary Ann loves the romance of the Victorian era. For this piece her husband Ken created a custom chain design that he calls 'Closed Box' and Mary Ann wanted to make a significant piece from metal clay to complement it. Mary Ann comments, "This garden box is a hollow form embellished with 3 dichroic glass cabochons. The top of the box has an orchid and every side of the box is sculptural."

Physical Attributes

- Pendant:
  1 1/4" (3.2 cm) High
  1 1/2" (3.8 cm) Long
  3/4" (19 mm) Wide
- Necklace (Overall):
  22" (56 cm) Cord Length
  9" (23 cm) Hanging Length

Materials & Components

- Lump, Paste & Syringe clay
- Lab Grown Sapphire
- Dichroic Glass Cabochon
- Sterling Silver Wire

Dichro Eternity
Silver & Dichroic Glass Pendant

Mary Ann Devos
Fort Myers Beach, Florida USA
www.silverclayworks.com

Ken Devos, (Sterling Silver Chain)
Fort Myers Beach, Florida USA
www.silverclayworks.com

Mary Ann often takes her inspiration clues from the components that she intends to incorporate into her piece. The artist comments, "After I had the glass cabochon and Ken's chain on hand I knew that the design of my pendant had to reflect the circular spiral theme. This classic shaped pendant takes a large measure of its dazzle from colors in the dichroic glass."

Physical Attributes
- Pendant:
  1 3/4" (4.4 cm) High
  1" (2.5 cm) Wide
  1/4" (6 mm) Thick
- Necklace (Overall):
  20" (51 cm) Cord Length
  8 1/2" (21.6 cm) Hanging Length

Materials & Components
- Lump, Paste & Syringe clay
- Dichroic Glass Cabochon
- Glass Beads
- Sterling Silver Wire

Inner City Blues
Locket Box Pendant

Mary Ellin D'Agostino
San Pablo, California USA
www.medacreations.com

Mary Ellin has striven to explore human nature and expressions of culture in her career as an artist, anthropologist, and archaeologist. The city or civilization is an ongoing theme in her work and this pendant unites a rectilinear city motif with a half-rounded 3-D box. Blue enamel was blended into the metal clay in varying concentrations and used to form the buildings. This hybrid material lends itself well to this artist's sculptural approach to jewelry making.

These views from the front show the top in open position to reveal more cityscape.

Physical Attributes

- Pendant
  2 3/4" (7 cm) High
  1 1/2 (3.8 cm) Wide
  3/4" (19 mm) Deep (lid closed)
  1 1/2" (3.8 cm) Diameter (lid opened)
- Necklace (Overall):
  24" (61 cm) Chain Length
  10 1/2" (27 cm) Hanging Length

Materials & Components

- Lump clay & Paste clay
- Fine silver wire
- Sterling Silver neck chain
- Glass Enamel
- Patina

Exceptional Works in Metal Clay & Glass

Glassberry Fruit
Glass Bead with Silver Tracery Pendant

Heather Fairfield

Woodstock, Connecticut USA
http://heather-fairfield.tripod.com

Heather used black soda-lime glass to create the cabochon that is the central component in this pendant. She added the metal clay syringe work and the slab formed leaves in separate fabrication steps.

Front side of pendant

Reverse side of pendant

Physical Attributes

- Pendant:
  1" (2.5 cm) Wide
  2 3/4" (7 cm) Long
  1/2" (13 mm) Thick
- Necklace (Overall):
  21" (53 cm) Chain Length
  10" (25 cm) Hanging Length

Materials & Components

- Lump, Paste, & Syringe clay
- Soda-lime glass cabochon
- Fine silver bail
- Fine silver chain

Summer Garden
Glass Encased Silverwork

Patsy Evins
Hallettsville, Texas USA
www.patsyevinsstudio.com

Patsy strives to express her joys and loves in her art. One of her special techniques is to encase the silver in glass, to blur the boundaries between these two mediums. The inspiration for this necklace was the profusion of summer flowers that grow in her garden. A natural harmonious flow is expressed throughout the necklace, while each medium retains its innate characteristic.

Physical Attributes	Materials & Components
• Flower Pendant:	• Lump, Paste, & Syringe clay
1" (2.5 cm) High	• Soda-lime glass
2" (5.1 cm) Wide	• Borocillicate glass
• Necklace (Overall):	• Silver wire
21" (53 cm) Bead String Length	• Asstd. Pearls & Seed beads
9 1/4" (23 cm) Hanging Length	

Orchid Bloom
Glass Encased Silverwork

Patsy Evins
Hallettsville, Texas USA
www.patsyevinsstudio.com

Christopher Evins
Silversmithing
Hallettsville, Texas USA

Patsy creates art in miniature form. Her mediums are glass and metal clay. The objective of this necklace is to artistically express a moment of beauty from nature. Patsy uses color-rich fibers, opulent pearls and delicate leaves to create an air of elegant lushness in support the regal orchid.

Physical Attributes	Materials & Components
• Flower Pendant:	• Lump, Paste, & Syringe clay
1" (2.5 cm) High	• Soda-lime glass
2" (5.1 cm) Wide	• Silver & Gold wire
• Necklace (Overall):	• Knitting fibers
23" (58 cm) Bead String Length	• Asstd. Pearls & Seed beads
10" (25 cm) Hanging Length	

Ocean Life
Glass Encased Silverwork

Patsy Evins
Hallettsville, Texas USA
www.patsyevinsstudio.com

Patsy sculpts her art using glass and metal clay. Creating art to showcase as well as wear is her earnest aspiration. This necklace embodies the full spectrum of 'Ocean Life' in all its exotic diversity. Close inspection of this piece reveals fish, sea anemones, coral and more. The effect is a beautiful, watery universe in jewel-toned hues with an ebb and flow perception.

This image shows the metal clay 'Fish Motif' necklace clasp.

The necklace detail features a blow fish, coral, and more.

Physical Attributes

- Flower Pendant:
  1" (2.5 cm) High
  2" (5.1 cm) Wide
- Necklace (Overall):
  25" (63 cm) Bead String Length
  11" (28 cm) Hanging Length

Materials & Components

- Lump, Paste, & Syringe clay
- Soda-lime glass
- Borocillicate glass
- Silver wire
- Asstd. Pearls, Seed beads and other commercial glass beads

A Dream of Silence
Cylindrical Box with Hinged Lid

Jonna Faulkner

La Jolla, California USA
www.exceptionalworks.net/faulkner

Jenny Friske-Baer (Glass Ornament on Box)

Eugene, Oregon USA
www.divinesparkdesigns.com

Metal clay is the primary medium Jonna uses to create jewelry and small objets d'art. She notes, "When my work is going really well, it feels like I've tapped into an alternate reality and pieces emerge organically rather than under the direction of my conscious mind and that happened with this project". Jenny's Lampworked glass ornament inspired the oceanic theme of this creation in the form of a box with a hinged lid. The interior 'tide pool' reflects her love of hidden treasures and miniature things.

Box lid in open position

Box bottom (lid closed)

Physical Attributes

- 1" (2.5 cm) High
- 1 3/8" (3.5 cm) Diameter

Materials & Components

- Lump, Paste, Syringe & Paper clay
- Lampworked glass
- Sterling Silver wire
- Pearl & Garnets

Emerald Bowl

Silver & Glass Enamel Bowl

Gaby Friberg

Uppsala, Sweden
www.exceptionalworks.net/friberg

Gaby has dedicated this piece to her late father as a thank you for the knowledge and inspiration he gave her during his long life as an enamellist and goldsmith. The artist comments, "Enameling is what I enjoyed the most when working with him in his workshop." The bowl could be a baptism gift or an evening place for wedding rings or just to put on display. There is a faint pattern in the silver to enhance the translucent enamel and to represent the hammer marks from making a bowl in the traditional way. The glass enamel is applied in multiple layers using several colors making it one-of-a-kind.

Physical Attributes

- 1 3/16" (3 cm) Diameter
- 13/16" (2 cm) High

Materials & Components

- Lump & Paste clay
- Glass Enamels

Midsummer

Silver & Cubic Zirconia Tiara

Gaby Friberg

Uppsala, Sweden
www.exceptionalworks.net/friberg

Midsummer night is the shortest night of the year in Sweden - in Uppsala (near Stockholm) it is daylight for almost 23 hours. All the flowers are blooming and tradition dictates that the girls and young women are supposed to pick seven of the most beautiful wild flowers and lay them under their pillows with the hope that their future husband will appear to them in a dream. Gaby's tiara has seven large flowers (2 flowers are hidden around the corners) and fourteen smaller flowers to denote the correct number for the girls to collect. In addition there are 21 smaller flowers on the backside of the tiara.

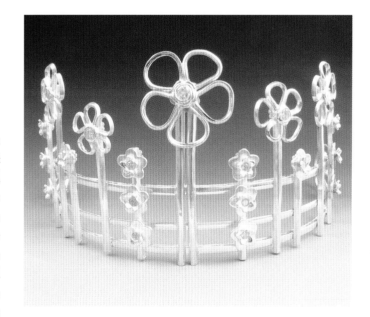

Physical Attributes

- 6 1/2" (16.5 cm) Long
- 4" (10.2 cm) High
- 5 1/8" (13 cm) Deep

Materials & Components

- Lump & Paste clay
- Cubic Zirconia

Venetian Star

Glass Beads & Silver Bracelet

Sherry Fotopoulos
San Antonio, Texas USA
www.pmc123.com

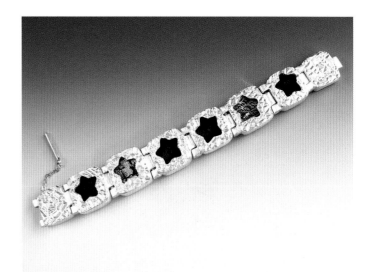

Sherry brings a wealth of art education and creative experience to her work as sculptor and metal-smith. During a stay in Venice, Italy Sherry purchased several strands of glass beads. She comments, "Every time I looked at those beads, memories of color, variety and craftsmanship that I experienced in Venice came flooding back". Each square bead has a slightly different shape and Sherry had to create an investment model for each one so she could create the unique presentation setting for the bead. Her goal was to create a simple bracelet that was tailored to allow each bead to tell its own story.

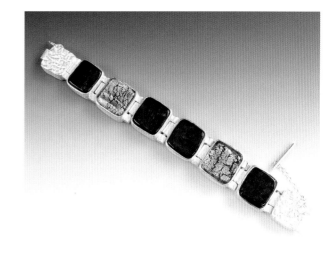

Physical Attributes

- 5/16" (8 mm) High
- 3/4" (19 mm) Wide
- 7 1/2" (19.1 cm) Long

Materials & Components

- Lump & Paste clay
- Venetian glass beads
- Fine Silver
- Sterling Silver chain

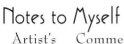

Sherry Fotopoulos
San Antonio, Texas USA
www.pmc123.com

Notes to Myself

Artist's Commentary: "My daughter Franki has always been my best critic. When I'm troubled during the realization of a piece she knows whether to encourage me to persevere or to let go and move on. That's when I make 'Notes to Myself.'"

Physical Attributes

- 11" (28 cm) High,
- 4 1/2" (11.4 cm) Wide

Materials & Components

- Lump & Paste clay
- Glass enamel
- Wood pencil & Human hair

Physical Attributes

- 15" (38 cm) High
- 1/2" (13 mm) Wide

Materials & Components

- Lump & Paste clay
- Glass enamel
- Wood handle & Human hair

Self Portrait

Artist's Commentary: "If I were an artist's tool, what would I look like? I have acquired a few life impressions, developed opinions and learned many skills. I like to think of my spirit as tall, slender and sturdy. Perhaps this would be my 'Self Portrait.'"

Goddess

Artist's Commentary: "My daughter Tina changed my life when she bore my grandson Nicos Alexander. Full and fecund, with lush luxuriant dark hair and crystal-clear blue eyes. There lay a mother and son, a living 'Goddess!'"

Physical Attributes

- 10" (25.4 cm),
- 4 1/2" (11.4 cm) Wide

Materials & Components

- Lump & Paste clay
- Glass enamel
- Animal horn & Human hair

Sisters (In Memory of Joanne)

Fine Silver and Dichroic Pendant

Donna Fox
Sydney, New South Wales Australia
www.sympatica.com.au

Donna admits to having a love of glass for most of her adult life working for the past 10 years in traditional stained glass, lampworking and fusing. This piece is dedicated to the memory of her sister Joanne. The twin dichroic focal points are symbolic of two sisters, alike in so many ways yet different to the eye. The base of the pendant is a hollow box construction that is not single dimensional (sisters relationships are anything but) with a texture on the back to symbolize the fabric of our lives that held us together.

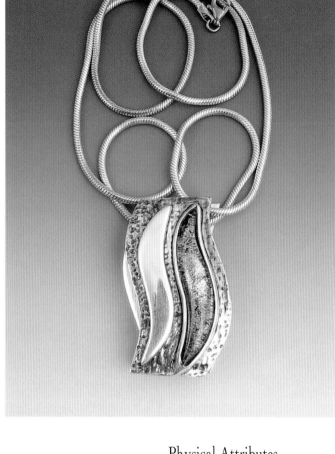

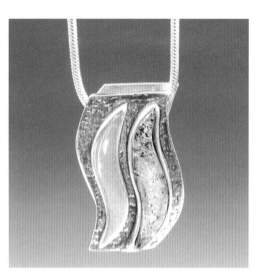

Physical Attributes

- Pendant
  1 5/8" (4.1 cm) High
  1 1/16" (17 mm) Wide
  3/16" (5 mm) Thick
- Necklace (Overall):
  24" (61 cm) Chain Length
  13 3/8" (34 cm) Hanging Length

Materials & Components

- Lump & Paste clay
- Dichroic fused glass
- Silver rope chain

Dots & Dots Ring
Silver & Flameworked Glass Bead

Barbara Becker Simon
Cape Coral, Florida USA
www.bbsimon.com

Barbara has been a jeweler for over thirty-five years. In addition to her metalwork she has gained a national reputation for her lampworked glass beads. The artist comments, "When introduced to the world of lampworking I was gleefully consumed with the drive to create small, intimate objects in glass. Manipulating hot glass is, for me, an exciting and joyful process. When I can combine my glass with my metalwork, I feel that the best of both worlds has been achieved." The 'Interchangeable Bead Ring' shown here has a stainless steel screw that was implanted into the body of the ring during the fabrication process. The locknut cap is a stainless steel nut that was covered and decorated with metal clay and fired. Barbara has made several beads that fit this ring allowing the wearer the opportunity to interchange the bead to match the occasion.

Physical Attributes

- Ring with Bead
  1 3/4" (4.4 cm) High
  1 1/4" (3.2 cm) Wide
- Glass Bead (only)
  5/8" (16 mm) High
  1" (2.5 cm) Wide

Materials & Components

- Lump & Paste clay
- Glass Bead
- Stainless Steel

Sedona Sunrise
Wire Wrapped Bead & Silver Necklace

Ruth Greening
Olympia, Washington USA
www.exceptionalworks.net/greening

Ruth's versatility and creativity allows her to make her unique artworks by combining several craft disciplines. For this piece she used the skills of lampworking, metal clay, chain mail, wire wrapping, and beading. The inspiration for this piece came from the bead itself, Ruth comments "When I took this bead from the annealing kiln I did not expect to find those wonderful streaks of color. I was transported to a warm southwestern desert at sunrise. The concept of hugging the bead with silver presented a fun challenge."

Reverse side of pendant shown above.

Physical Attributes

- Bead Pendant:
  3" (7.6 cm) High
  2" (5.1 cm) Wide
  3/4" (19 mm) Thick
- Necklace (Overall):
  25" (63 cm) Bead String Length
  15" (38 cm) Hanging Length

Materials & Components

- Lump & Paste (silver & 22K gold) clay
- Effetre Hollow Glass Bead
- Sterling silver wire & jump rings
- Hill Tribe silver beads
- Jasper beads

Sunny Clematis Vessel
Fine Silver & Effetre Glass Sculpture

Kaleigh Hessel
Cary North Carolina USA
www.flamekissedbeads.com

Kaleigh is a metalsmith and glass artist. She has developed a method of firing the metal clay to her hollow effetre glass (soda lime soft glass) bead vessels. This sculptural piece is one of several inspired by the many clematis vines the artist passes on her walks throughout her North Carolina neighborhood. Kaleigh comments, "In general much of my work is inspried by the colors and textures I find in nature".

Physical Attributes

- 2 5/16" (6.2 cm) High
- 1 1/16" (2.6 cm) Diameter

Materials & Components

- Lump, Paste & Syringe clay
- Effetre glass bead
- Quartz bead
- Silver chain

These 3 images above show the sculpture from various side and back views.

Promise of Spring

Silver, Glass & Wire Sculpture

Peggy A Houchin

Loveland, Colorado USA
www.bellabeadsandwax.com

Peggy has been designing & creating wearable art using mixed media for over 20 years. This sculpture combines metal clay with fine silver wire and glass enamels. The artist comments, "Your creativity should always be inspired by what you love. I had an idea to create these small metal clay flower vases using hollow forms then tied them together with a metal clay coil ribbon. The flowers are fine silver wire with a ball end that was dipped in assorted colors of glass enamels, perfect for the flower embellishments to add a touch of color to the sculpture."

Physical Attributes

- 2 1/2" (6.4 cm) High
- 2 1/2" (6.4 cm) Wide
- 1/2" (13 mm) Thick

Materials & Components

- Lump & Paste clay
- Fine silver wire
- Glass Enamels

Shaman of the Sea
Opal stone, Glass & Metal Clay Necklace

Jay Humphreys
Tucson, Arizona USA
www.metalclayveneer.com

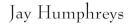

Jay's unique art springs from a myriad of experiences and sources. Her diverse images reflect a microbiologist's fascination with the miniscule, a nature lover's appreciation of the Arizona desert and a potter's obsession with clay. The artist comments, "My shaman is dressed in a thin layer of metal clay veneer. Arm over her heart, she gathers her coat of gold and silver. Her opal face reflects the mystery of the oceans with sparkle of the sun and light. Her hair of seaweeds drapes around her shoulders as she gathers trophies from the turbulent sea.

Physical Attributes

- Pendant:
  4" (10.2 cm) High
  4" (10.2 cm) Circumference
  1 1/4" (3.2 cm) Thick
- Necklace (Overall):
  20" (51 cm) Bead String Length
  12" (30 cm) Hanging Length

Materials & Components

- Paper & Syringe clay
- Paste clay (in silver & 22K gold)
- Opal stone
- Glass Beads
- Amethyst chips

Pansy Spoon
Silver & Plique-à-jour Enamel Sculpture

Louis Kappel
Belleville, Illinois USA
www.exceptionalworks.net/kappel

When Louis first encountered the plique-à-jour technique (French for 'open to light'), he knew he had to incorporate it into his work. The technique produces a transparent 'stained glass' effect where the silver is the 'lines' and the colored enamel is the 'glass'. The enamel is not applied to the surface of the silver instead it fills the open spaces in the lace-like design and held in place by surface tension until hardened during firing. In this piece the spoon base and cup were formed separately. The cup was syringed flat, shaped using a damping block then attached to the base with paste clay and fired. The enamel plique-à-jour was applied and fired as a final step.

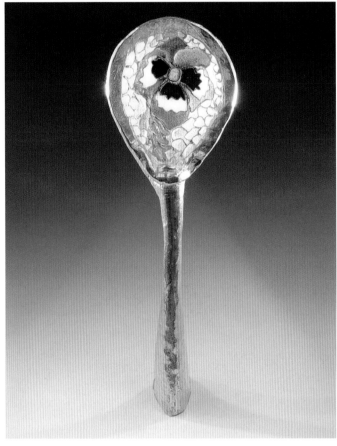

Image above is the back side of the spoon, viewing slightly down from above.

Image at right is a view from the front side of the spoon with front lighting to show the silver lace work more clearly.

Physical Attributes

- 4 1/16" (10.3 cm) Long
- 1 3/8" (3.5 cm) Wide
- 5/16" (8 mm) Thick

Materials & Components

- Lump, Paste & Syringe clay
- Transparent Glass Enamels

Louis Kappel
Belleville, Illinois USA
www.exceptionalworks.net/kappel

Louis wanted to make a vessel with a flower motif where the cup would comprise the flowers and the leaves while the vessel's stem and base would represent the stem and roots of the plant. Louis used the plique-à-jour technique (French for 'open to light') to create the transparent colored flowers and leaves seen in the cup (see Louis' Pansy Spoon on page 40 for a description of the plique-à-jour technique). The effect of the colorful cup mounted on the sculpted stem and root base is striking.

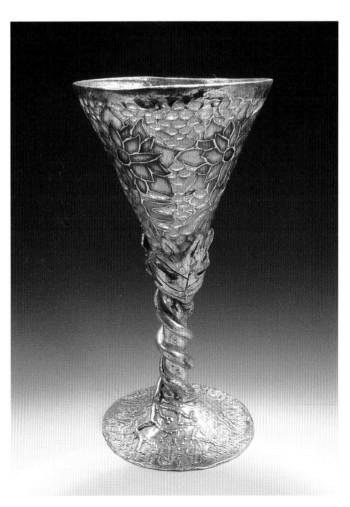

Physical Attributes

- 5" (12.7 cm) High
- 2 9/16" (6.5 cm) Diameter

Materials & Components

- Lump, Paste & Syringe clay
- Transparent Glass Enamels

S wim to the Top
Silver & Dichroic Glass Pendant

Linda Kline
Vero Beach, Florida USA
www.lindaklinedesigns.com

Elisa Cossey, (Dichroic Glass Cabochon)
Blanchard, Oklahoma USA
www.elisacossey.com

Linda's one-of-a-kind jewelry, sculpture & wearable art are created with a message. The artist comments, "I want my work to have a voice - to create something that's not only beautiful but that also tells a story and hopefully make someone think." This pendant features a dichroic glass cabochon with incredible blue orbs and a foam-like foreground that provided a compliment to the artist's design concept. The silver marine life elements were individually hand sculpted. A patina was added to darken the valleys and create depth and dimension.

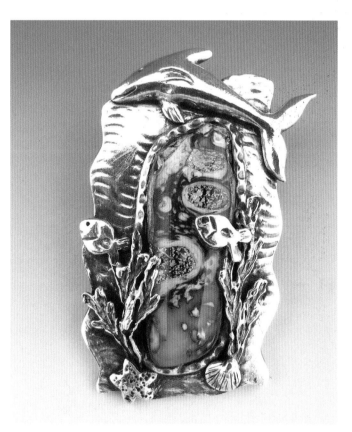

Physical Attributes

- 2 1/2" (6.4 cm) Long
- 1 1/4" (3.2 cm) Wide
- 5/16" (8 mm) Thick

Materials & Components

- Lump, Paste & Syringe clay
- Dichroic Glass Cabochon
- Glass Enamels

Over the Hole &
The Blue Hole

Silver Pendant with Enamel Bowl

Linda Kline
Vero Beach, Florida USA
www.lindaklinedesigns.com

Linda's 'Sea Life in a Whole New Way' series (that includes this piece and the pendant on page 42) were inspired by a trip the artist took to Belize. Linda comments. "I was diving in a place called the 'Blue Hole' that is an amazing phenomenon. It appears to be virtually bottomless with a surreal deep blue color and an abundance of marine life." This piece is decorative, functional, and wearable art - all in one. The 'Blue Hole' is an enameled bowl and the pendant necklace doubles as a lid 'Over the Hole' when it is in storage.

Physical Attributes

- Pendant:
  1 5/8" (4.1 cm) Diameter
  3/8" (10 mm) Thick
- Necklace (Overall):
  26" (66 cm) Chain Length
  11" (28 cm) Hanging Length
- Bowl (with lid in place):
  1 5/8" (4.1 cm) Diameter
  1 1/4" (3.2 cm) Tall

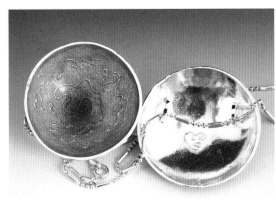

Materials & Components

- Lump, Paste & Syringe clay
- Glass Enamels
- Sterling Silver Chain

Coterie (wing)
Lampworked Bead & Silver Ring

Sara Sally LaGrand

Lenexa, Kansas USA
www.prettybabiesglass.com

Sara strives to achieve objects that appeal and amuse. She comments, "Nothing is off limits in terms of personal adornment. I love to combine unusual materials with the metal clay and glass to provide a sense of an earthy yet ethereal connection. I like to think of myself as a co-creator with the forces of nature." The guinea feathers in 'Coterie' (meaning wing) provided the design inspiration for each part of the assemblage, from the décor on the bead to the masked dots on the interior of the ring. Each angle offers a little surprise for the viewer in a satisfyingly unusual way.

Physical Attributes

- Overall Assembly:
  1 1/2" (3.8 cm) Tall
  1 1/4" (3.2 cm) Wide
- Bead (upper only):
  1 1/4" (3.2 cm) Diameter
  1/2" (13 mm) High
- Ring (lower only):
  11/16" (18 mm) Diameter

Materials & Components

- Lump, Paste & Sheet clay
- Lampworked Glass Bead
- Fine Silver Wire
- Feathers

Contemporary Rings
Silver & Glass Rod Rings

Pat Lasater

Fort Worth, Texas USA
www.exceptionalworks.net/lasater

Pat has a passion for rings. She recently added colorful glass rods to her art material selection and the two rings presented here are the result of that blending. The artist comments, "The most exciting part of working with metal clay and glass is that you are never completely sure what the end results will be."

Physical Attributes

- Overall Assembly:
  1 1/8" (2.9 cm) Tall
  7/8" (22 mm) Wide
- Ring only:
  7/8" (22 mm) Diameter

Materials & Components

- Lump & Paste clay
- Glass Rod

The Sun Warms the City

Silver & Glass Enamel Dish

Jeanette Landenwitch

Florence, Kentucky USA
www.jmlcreations.com

Jeanette's concept for this design was to symbolize the strength and power of nature. The image of the sun is central and much larger than the city, represented by the small gold squares. The background texture shows the ocean shore and the various shades of lighter blues signify daytime while the darker purples suggest the darkness of night. The silver dish was freeform shaped, the gold coil was added and it was fired. The gold squares for the 'city' and the central sun motif were cut and fired separately. A few layers of glass enamel were applied then the gold 'city & sun' components were set and fired.

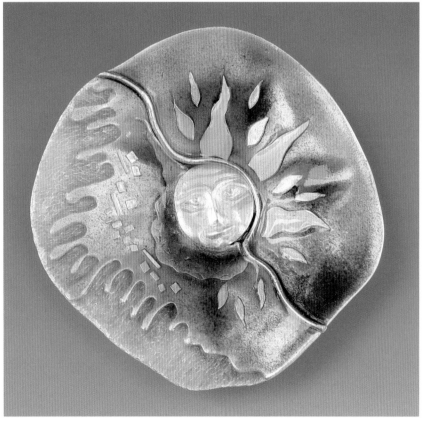

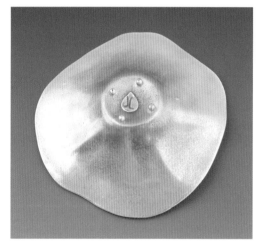

Physical Attributes

- 3" (7.6 cm) Diameter
- 3/4" (19 mm) High

Materials & Components

- Lump & Paste clay – silver
- Lump & Sheet clay – 22K gold
- Glass Enamels

Budding Vase
Silver & Plique-à-jour Enamel Vessel

Jeanette Landenwitch
Florence, Kentucky USA
www.jmlcreations.com

Jeanette's designs are often inspired by her love of gardening, flowers and nature in general. The sculpture's shape is reminiscent of the flowing shapes of petals, leaves and stems and the colors are those that occur naturally in the flowers. Jeanette was looking for a challenge and decided this vessel would be her opportunity to push the limits of her experience with the plique-à-jour technique - French for 'open to light' (see page 41 & 41 for other examples of this technique. Since the vessel was curved the method of enamel application had to be by surface tension alone (no backing). The larger cells called for patience and multiple firing (approximately 35 in all) but the results are a stunning testament to the perseverance for meeting a challenge.

Physical Attributes

- 3 3/4" (9.5 cm) Tall
- 1 1/4" (3.2 cm) wide

Materials & Components

- Lump, Paste & Syringe clay
- Transparent Glass Enamels

Jeweled Vessel

Ceramic, Glass & Silver Sculpture

Vera Lightstone
New York, New York USA
www.silverclay.com

Vera has worked and taught sculptural media for years, ranging from large ceramic sculpture to graceful vessels, from unusual silver jewelry to arresting mounted silver sculpture. In this work the ceramic vessel, the silver adornments and the dichroic glass are fired and finished separately. They are then assembled and fired together. The artist is delighted to follow the ancient tradition of jeweled vessels using 21st century materials. The artist comments, "My work draws its inspiration from nature. To enhance such a humble practical piece – a pot after all – I chose to refer to forest leaves sparkling with the natural jewels of early morning dew."

Physical Attributes

- 5 1/4" (13.3 cm) Tall
- 2 1/4" (5.7 cm) Wide
- 1 1/4" (3.2 cm) Deep

Materials & Components

- Lump, Paste & Syringe clay
- Fired & Glazed Stoneware
- Dichroic Glass Cabochons

Seascape

Ceramic, Glass & Silver Sculpture

Vera Lightstone
New York, New York USA
www.silverclay.com

Vera had been a ceramic sculptor for many years before she was introduced and inspired by the alchemy of turning a clay-like material into silver and she has been combining these two mediums ever since. This tray-form piece was first sculpted, glazed and fired. Likewise the silver & glass adornments were also created and fired separately. Vera comments, "My experiences diving in the warm blue waters of the Caribbean inspired this piece. I used dichroic glass gems to represent the sparkling sea bottom then molded silver sea creatures to complete this watery seascape."

Physical Attributes

- 1" (2.5 cm) Tall
- 5 1/4" (13.3 cm) Wide
- 4 1/2" (11.4 cm) Deep

Materials & Components

- Lump, Paste & Syringe clay
- Fired & Glazed Stoneware
- Dichroic Glass Cabochons

A Native Affair
Silver & Glass Enamel Pendant

Donna Lewis

Scottsdale, Arizona USA
www.exceptionalworks.net/lewis

Donna combines glass enamels and metal clay with a purpose to create pools of pure color in each piece. Donna comments, "I feel amazingly satisfied with the interaction between certain hues and the pureness of fine silver. For this piece I wanted to create the sense of Native American jewelry. The colors, the expression and the sky-earth relationship."

Physical Attributes

- Pendant:
  2 1/8" (5.4 cm) Diameter
  5/8" (16 mm) Thick
- Necklace (Overall):
  19" (48 cm) Bead String Length
  8 1/2" (21.5 cm) Hanging Length

Materials & Components

- Lump, Paste & Syringe clay
- Glass Enamels
- Cubic zirconia stone
- Necklace:
- Glass & Crystal Beads
- Freshwater Pearls
- Sterling Silver components

Spy With My Little Eye
Silver Fused Glass Pendant

Kurt Madison
Greenacres, Washington USA
www.punctumstudios.com

Kurt is continually collecting found objects, experimenting with glass and working with other materials to create parts for his pieces. He calls this treasure trove his 'bench collection' out of which many of his finished works evolve. For instance, the red glass for this piece originally came from a glass blower friend and was slump-fused by Kurt a few years ago. The artist comments, "I recently saw the glass as a hood or a veil and the title just came to mind – I call this a 'thunder-strike' design process." The eye was formed with lump clay and a triangle CZ and that was fitted to the glass and fired. The piece was further decorated with syringe work and gold paste overlay. Five separate firings were required to complete the work.

Physical Attributes

- Pendant:
  3" (7.6 cm) High
  2 1/4" (5.7 cm) Wide
  5/8" (16 mm) Thick
- Necklace (Overall):
  22" (56 cm) Chain Length
  10 1/2" (27 cm) Hanging Length

Materials & Components

- Lump, Paste & Syringe clay – silver
- Paste clay – gold
- Fused Glass medallion
- Cubic zirconia stone
- Fine silver wire & necklace chain
- Sterling Silver & tube

Bobèche

Fine Silver & Beach Glass

Tim McCreight

Portland, Maine USA
www.brynmorgen.com

Tim is a metalsmith, designer, author, and teacher who has been working in metals since 1970. A bobèche is an ornamental element that fits on a tapered candle to catch dripping wax. For this piece Tim started by creating 4" (10 cm) disks shaped over a 10" (25 cm) children's playground ball. When the disks were dry they were sanded and 2 disks were attached to create a hollow saucer shape. Sections were cut away to hold the various pieces of beach glass. The central hole has an internal rim fabricated from fine silver and soldered as a final step. The artist comments, "One of the pleasures of using beach glass is the fact that I never know what color it will be when it emerges from the kiln. In addition, I like the idea of transforming a discarded scrap into a focal point on an elegant piece."

View of bobèche top surface

Bobèche underside

Physical Attributes

- 4" (10.2 cm) Diameter (silver saucer)
- 5" (12.7 cm) Wide (outer glass edge)
- 1/2" (13 mm) Deep (at center rim)

Materials & Components

- Lump & Paste clay
- Beach Glass Cabochons
- Fine silver

Ocean Life

Glass & Silver Pendant

Tami R Morrison
Houston, Texas USA
www.moasidesigns.com

Glynna White, (Dichroic Glass Cabochon)
Spring, Texas USA
www.beadoholique.com

Tami designs classic and contemporary metal clay jewelry and sculptures. Using glass, whether in enamel or cabochon form, is one of Tami's favorite ways to add a colorful focal point to a piece. The artist comments, "The idea for this piece came quite by accident, as this cabochon was initially intended for a ring. I wrapped the bezel and while it was drying I started experimenting with my new clay extruder. The extrusions reminded me of jellyfish tendrils. Needless to say when I thought of the sea colored cabochon that I had just prepared, the idea for 'Ocean Life' was born."

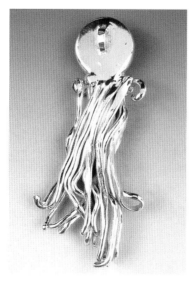

Physical Attributes

- 2 1/2" (6.4 cm) Long
- 1" (2.5 cm) Wide
- 1/2" (13 mm) Thick

Materials & Components

- Lump & Paste clay
- Dichroic Cabochon
- Fine silver bail

Silverglyph
Silver with Fused & Shaped Glass

Jayne Persico
Hazleton, Pennsylvania USA
www.jpglassworks.com

Jayne has been designing and creating glass jewelry for many years. She is best known for her innovative 'Kiln Formed Bracelet' technique that she used to create this piece. Jayne has developed many styles of glass bracelets and is currently embellishing her cuffs with silver elements. The artist comments, "Designing glass jewelry is my passion. While the kiln formed bracelet process has always been personally gratifying for me, I still continue to explore new design challenges. Incorporating metal clay into my work is an excellent example of this challenge. The temperature at which a bracelet is manipulated and the maturing temperature of low fired metal clay are perfectly suited"

Physical Attributes

- 2 5/8" (6.7 cm) Long
- 2 1/4" (5.7 cm) High
- 1" (2.5 cm) Wide

Materials & Components

- Lump clay
- Fused & Formed Glass Bracelet

Purple Passion

Silver, Glass & Slate Pendant

Sally Spencer
Didcot, Oxon, United Kingdom
www.jewellerybysallyjane.co.uk

Sally's love of the art nouveau period is echoed within her individual jewelry designs that explore and delight in the fluid and organic nature of metal clay. The combination of glass, silver and Welsh slate in this pendant illustrates her continuing passion for experimenting in combining metal clay with other materials. Sally comments, "A visit to the National Slate Museum in Wales prompted me to explore using slate in my work. I love the dark, matt contrast with the brightness of the silver. This pendant allowed me to indulge my love of color using the glass, the natural world with the slate and silver jewelry – three things that I am passionate about."

Physical Attributes
- Pendant:
  1 7/8" (4.8 cm) Long
  1 1/16" (2.8 cm) Wide
  7/8" (22 mm) Thick
- Necklace (Overall):
  20" (51 cm) Cord Length
  9 3/4" (25 cm) Hanging Length

Materials & Components
- Lump, Paste & Syringe clay
- Dichroic Fused Glass
- Cubic Zirconia
- Welsh Slate
- Leather Cord necklace
- Fine Silver wire

Whimsical Jester
Ring with Spinning Bead

Hattie Sanderson
Clare, Illinois USA
www.exceptionalworks.net/sanderson

This ring is the artist's whimsical interpretation of a jester. This project required careful pre-planning and creation of several separate metal clay components. The pieces were then fitted together with paste clay and fired. The final assembly involved the installation of a row of small beads plus a larger handmade bead that had to fit the space perfectly to allow it to spin freely.

Photography on this page by Hattie Sanderson

Physical Attributes

- Physical Attributes
- 1 5/8" (4.1 cm) High
- 1 1/8" (2.9 cm) Wide (at beads)
- 1" (2.5 cm) Diameter (at the base)

Materials & Components

- Lump clay & Paste clay
- Fine Silver wire
- Lampworked Glass Bead (feature bead)
- Small Glass and Silver Beads

Tracery Beads & Shield
Openwork Silver Bead Pendant

Hattie Sanderson
Clare, Illinois USA
www.exceptionalworks.net/sanderson

The metal clay beads were made using a 'Pro Bead Roller' and wood clay armatures. Several separate metal clay components work together to form the complete structure of this comprehensive fabrication that includes glass beads, silver beads & bead caps, a clay shield and coin medallion. The pendant is mounted permanently on a string of blue glass beads.

Photography on this page by Hattie Sanderson

Physical Attributes

- Large silver Beads:
  1 3/8" (3.5 cm) High
  5/8" (16 mm) Wide
- Silver Shield:
  1 3/8" (3.5 cm) Wide
  1" (2.5 cm) High
- Glass Beads:
  7/8" (22 mm) Diameter

Materials & Components

- Lump clay & Paste clay
- Fine Silver wire
- Lampworked Glass Beads
- Glass Bead Necklace

Garden Party

Silver & Glass Enamel Sculpture

Leslie Tieke

Seymour, Tennessee USA
www.tieke.net

Leslie believes that one should enjoy the process and adventure of creating unique pieces that lead you in new directions and discovery as an artist. In other words, play! Leslie has been a metal clay instructor for many years and has amassed a large collection of class demonstration pieces. This sculpture is the end result of the assembly of these pieces in one 3-D collage. The artist comments, "I did not have a preconceived idea when I started this sculpture; I simply let the individual pieces take me to the 'Garden Party'. As the work progressed a 'Moon Family' theme began to emerge with faces of various family members intermingled with stars, dragonflies and flowers – a party indeed!"

Physical Attributes

- 2 3/4" (7 cm) High
- 2 1/2" (6.4 cm) Wide
- 3 3/8" (8.6 cm) Long

Materials & Components

- Lump, Paste, Syringe & Sheet clay
- Fused Glass
- Glass Enamels
- Cubic Zirconia
- Fine Silver wire

Royal Treasure Box
Silver & Glass Sculpture

Jackie Truty
Oaklawn, Illinois USA
www.artclayworld.com

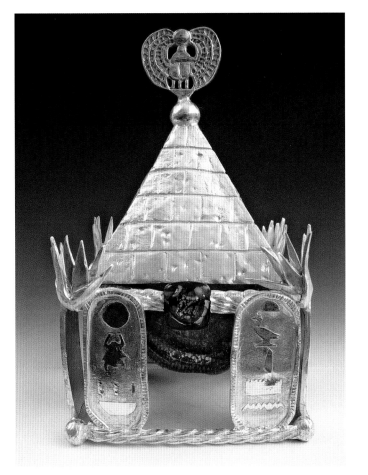

Jackie believes that metal clay and glass were made for each other. She comments, "I love creating pieces where there is a symbiosis of the two, where neither component is completely whole without the other." This 'Royal Treasure Box' takes its inspiration from Egypt's great kings and queens who left behind thousands of spectacular artifacts. The box is decorated with cartouches from several archeological treasures including Ramesses, Tutenkhamun, Nefertiti and others. The dichroic glass bowl that is inside the box was fused and slumped first. Then the metal clay frame was fabricated to fit around the glass and the whole assembly was fired.

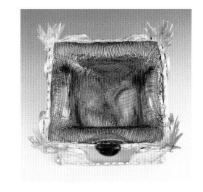

Physical Attributes

- Overall Box (with lid on):
  4 1/8" (10.5 cm) High
  2 3/4" (7 cm) Square
- Pyramid (including medallion):
  2 3/4" (7 cm) High
  2 3/8" (6 cm) Square

Materials & Components

- Lump, Paste & Syringe clay
- Dichroic Glass – Fused & Slumped

Grapevine Inro Pendant

Silver & Glass Box-type Pendant

Michela Verani

Londonderry, New Hampshire USA
www.everlastingtreasures.org

Michela enjoys making containers using metal clay. For this piece she decided to create a traditional Japanese Inro Pendant. Since kimonos have no pockets it was convenient to have a small container for personal items hung around the neck on a double cord. Michela decided to create her own 'Inro' interpretation in metal clay and glass. The artist comments, "I made some 'dichro-dots' for another project and moved the extras to one side, when I saw them clustered together they looked like a tiny bunch of grapes and I knew I had to add them to this piece."

Physical Attributes

- Pendant:
  1 1/2" (3.8 cm) High
  1" (2.5 cm) Wide
  1/2" (13 mm) Deep
- Necklace (Overall):
  26" (66 cm) Chain Length
  13 1/2" (34 cm) Hanging Length

Materials & Components

- Lump, Paste & Syringe clay – silver
- Dichroic Glass – Fused
- Sterling Silver wire & necklace chain

Blue Bug Brooch
Dichroic Glass & Silver Pin

Michela Verani
Londonderry, New Hampshire USA
www.everlastingtreasures.org

Michela's primary medium as an artist is silver metal clay, however finding other materials to add to the clay during firing is of great interest to her. Michela comments, "The sparkle and flash of dichroic glass called out to the 'magpie' in me and in the last year or so I have started to make my own cabochons and 'dichro-dots' to add to my metal clay pieces." The insect world has long fascinated Michela. Most people dislike bugs but they can be quite beautiful. The dichroic glass accents in this bug imparts an iridescent quality that makes it really come alive.

Physical Attributes

- 2" (5.1 cm) Long
- 3/4" (1.9 cm) Wide
- 1/2" (13 mm) Deep

Materials & Components

- Lump, Paste & Syringe clay
- Dichroic Glass – Fused
- Fine Silver pin findings

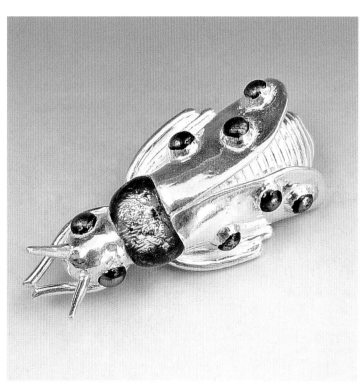

Summer's End
Slumped Glass & Silver Sculpture

Sherry Viktora

Rockton, Illinois USA
www.out-ona-limb.com

Sherry used a slag chunk of Fenton Art Glass to create a solid base for this sculpture. The slag glass was fire polished in her fusing kiln to smooth over the edges. Sherry comments, "I fabricated the base of the flower and the leaves by coating an actual hibiscus flower and leaves with paste clay." The petals of both flowers were cut and fused then slumped into the fired and polished silver bases. The shaping of the glass petals was done in another firing using hand-made refractory clay molds and a fiber blanket. The stems were formed using wood clay with additional sculpturing on the outside. The last step was to assemble all the components into the final sculpture.

Physical Attributes

- 4 1/2" (11.4 cm) High
- 6" (15.2 cm) Wide
- 6" (15.2 cm) Deep

Materials & Components

- Lump, Paste, Syringe & Sheet clay
- Fusible Sheet Glass and Frit
- Slag Glass Chunk
- Molding Material

Lampworked Glass & Silver Beads

Beth Williams

Gloucester, Maine USA
www.bethwilliams.com

Dark Blue Dream Pod

As both a glass beadmaker and metalsmith Beth's work includes jewelry, sculpture and home accents. Beth comments, "The idea of combining metals directly with lampworked glass became an obsession for me more than 15 years ago."

Physical Attributes

- 1 1/4" (3.2 cm) Long
- 1 1/4" (3.2 cm) Wide
- 1/2" (1.3 cm) Thick

Materials & Components

- Lump clay
- Fine Silver foil
- Lampworked Soft Glass

Green Tornado Bead

Beth continues, "The magical properties of metal clay allow me to work the two materials together, they play off each other in unexpected ways." The 2 beads represented here are indicative of the new direction that Beth is taking with her bead making, creating shaped hollow beads that reflect color and light and are accented with metal clay silver.

Physical Attributes

- 2 1/2" (6.4 cm) Long
- 3/4" (19 mm) Wide
- 1/2" (13 mm) Thick

Materials & Components

- Lump clay
- Fine Silver foil
- Lampworked Soft Glass

Wardell
PUBLICATIONS INC

Instruction, Inspiration and Innovation for the Art Glass Communnity

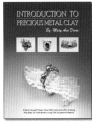  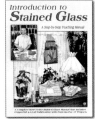   

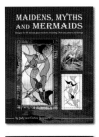     

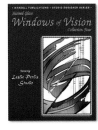    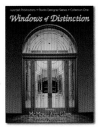 

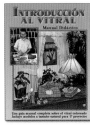  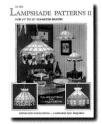   

e-mail: info@wardellpublications.com   website: www.wardellpublications.com